D0843322

Celebrations

Let's Get Ready for Easter

By Joanne Winne

Welcome
Books

Children's Press
A Division of Scholastic Inc.
New York / Toronto / London / Auckland / Sydney
Mexico City / New Delhi / Hong Kong
Danbury, Connecticut

Photo Credits: Cover, pp. 5, 7, 9, 13, 15, 17, 19, 21 by Maura Boruchow;
p. 11 © Arte & Immagini Srl/Corbis

Contributing Editor: Jennifer Silate
Book Design: Michael DeLisio

Visit Children's Press on the Internet at:
http://publishing.grolier.com

Library of Congress Cataloging-in-Publication Data

Winne, Joanne.
 Let's get ready for Easter / by Joanne Winne.
    p. cm. -- (Celebrations)
  Includes bibliographical references and index.
  ISBN 0-516-23172-3 (lib. bdg.) -- ISBN 0-516-29568-3 (pbk.)
  1. Easter--Juvenile literature. [1. Easter. 2. Holidays.] I. Title.

 GT4935 .W56 2001
 394.2667--dc21

                                          2001028095

Contents

We are getting ready for **Easter**.

We **dye** eggs to get ready for Easter.

I am dyeing this one green.

Look at the **calendar**.

Today is Easter.

9

On Easter, we celebrate the **rebirth** of Jesus Christ.

11

We wear our best clothes on Easter.

I wear a pretty hat.

On Easter, we get baskets filled with candy.

We like the **chocolate** best.

15

We are having an Easter egg hunt.

Can you find the egg?

We go to our grandparents' house for dinner.

19

Everything looks delicious.

Happy Easter!

21

New Words

calendar (**kal**-uhn-duhr) a chart showing the months, weeks, and days of the year

chocolate (**chahk**-uh-liht) a sweet made from roasted and ground cacao beans

dye (**dy**) to change the color of something

Easter (**ee**-stuhr) a Christian holiday celebrating Jesus Christ's return to life

rebirth (**ree**-berth) a new or second birth

To Find Out More

Books

An Easter Celebration: Traditions and Customs from Around the World
by Pamela Kennedy
Hambleton-Hill Publishing, Inc.

Easter
by Catherine Chambers
Raintree Steck-Vaughn Publishers

Web Site
Billy Bear's Happy Easter
http://www.billybear4kids.com/holidays/easter/fun.htm
On this Web site, you can color Easter pictures, play Easter games, learn Easter crafts, and much more.

Index

About the Author

Joanne Winne taught fourth grade for nine years. Now she writes and edits books for children. She lives in Hoboken, New Jersey.

Reading Consultants

Kris Flynn, Coordinator, Small School District Literacy, The San Diego County Office of Education

Shelly Forys, Certified Reading Recovery Specialist, W.J. Zahnow Elementary School, Waterloo, IL

Sue McAdams, Former President of the North Texas Reading Council of the IRA, and Early Literacy Consultant, Dallas, TX